IN THE ZONE

FIELD HOCKEY

JENNIFER HURTIG

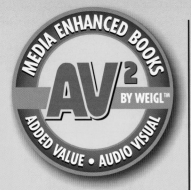

AV² provides enriched content that supplements and complements this book. Weigl's AV² books strive to create inspired learning and engage young minds in a total learning experience.

Your AV² Media Enhanced books come alive with...

Audio
Listen to sections of the book read aloud.

Key Words
Study vocabulary, and complete a matching word activity.

Video
Watch informative video clips.

Quizzes
Test your knowledge.

Embedded Weblinks
Gain additional information for research.

Slide Show
View images and captions, and prepare a presentation.

Try This!
Complete activities and hands-on experiments.

... and much, much more!

Go to **www.av2books.com**, and enter this book's unique code.

BOOK CODE

P217690

AV² by Weigl brings you media enhanced books that support active learning.

Download the AV² catalog at **www.av2books.com/catalog**

AV² Online Navigation on page 24

Published by AV² by Weigl
350 5th Avenue, 59th Floor
New York, NY 10118
Website: www.av2books.com   www.weigl.com

Library of Congress Cataloging-in-Publication Data
Hurtig, Jennifer.
Field hockey / Jennifer Hurtig.
   p. cm. -- (In the zone)
Includes index.
Summary: "Provides information about the fundamentals of field hockey, from equipment and moves to superstars and legends. Intended for third to fifth grade students"--Provided by publisher.
ISBN 978-1-62127-317-2 (hardcover : alk. paper) -- ISBN 978-1-62127-322-6 (softcover : alk. paper)
1. Field hockey--Juvenile literature. I. Title.
GV1017.H7H86 2013
796.355--dc23
                              2012044004

Printed in the United States in North Mankato, Minnesota
1 2 3 4 5 6 7 8 9 0   17 16 15 14 13

012013
WEP301112

PROJECT COORDINATOR Aaron Carr
EDITOR Steve Macleod
ART DIRECTOR Terry Paulhus

CONTENTS

What Is Field Hockey?

The word hockey probably comes from the French word *hoquet*, which means "shepherd's stick."

Field hockey is an ancient team sport. It dates back more than 4,000 years. Scientists found drawings of men playing hockey inside a tomb in Egypt.

There is also evidence of other ancient peoples playing this game, including American Indians. Field hockey used to only be played by men. Today, it is played by males and females of all ages.

The first men's field hockey club was formed in England. The club started in 1849. It was called Blackheath. The Hockey Association formed in London in 1886. The first women's club began the next year. The All England Women's Hockey Association was created in 1895. The sport quickly became popular with women.

Constance Applebee helped make field hockey popular in the United States. She was a gym teacher. She put on a field hockey demonstration in the summer of 1901. Field hockey is now an Olympic sport. Men began playing field hockey at the Olympics in 1908. Women began playing in 1980.

■ The field at the 2012 London Olympic Games was blue, so fans could see the ball more easily. It was the first Olympics to use a field that was not green.

The object of field hockey is to score goals. Players use hooked sticks to move the ball toward the goal.

Uniforms of the team's colors have a player's number on the back.

Players wear shin guards under their socks. The guards are made of plastic to protect players from sticks and balls.

Field hockey sticks can be made of wood. They can also be made of a fiberglass mixture. The sticks weigh between 19 and 24 ounces (539 and 680 grams). They vary in length. The sticks can be 31 to 38 inches (79 to 97 centimeters) long. Only the front of a field hockey stick is flat. The "toe" or "head" of the stick curves up.

Most field hockey balls are made of plastic. The balls are usually white. They are sometimes yellow or orange. They weigh about 5.5 ounces (156 g).

■ Field hockey players wear mouth guards to protect their teeth from balls and high sticks.

■ Players wear shoes with rubber bumps on the bottom, called turf shoes, when games are played on artificial turf. When outdoor games are played on grass, players wear cleats with metal or plastic spikes for better grip.

■ Female players often wear skirts as part of their uniform. Male players wear shorts.

F ield hockey can be played indoors or outdoors, though it is mostly played outside. Field hockey is played inside in some countries during winter.

An outdoor field is about twice the size of an indoor field. Outdoor fields are 100 yards (91.4 meters) long and 60 yards (55 m) wide. There is a goal cage at each end of the field. Outdoor cages are 7 feet (2.1 m) high and 12 feet (3.7 m) wide. Indoor cages are smaller. All fields are marked with a center line and **striking circles**. Outdoor fields also have a 25-yard (23 m) line on each half.

■ The ball can roll out of bounds in outdoor field hockey. Indoor fields have sideboards that keep the ball in play.

Outdoor Field

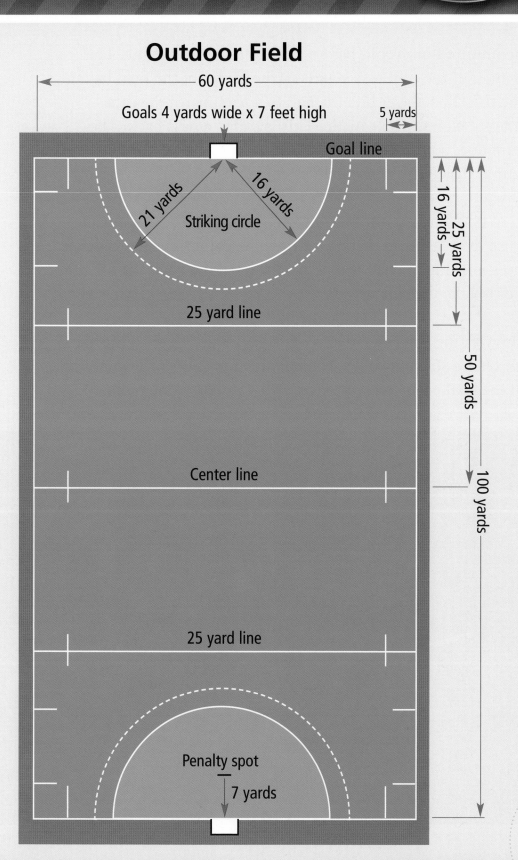

Field Hockey Basics

The **umpire** flips a coin before the beginning of a game. The winner of the coin toss stands in the center of the field facing the ball. The player hits the ball to a teammate when the umpire blows their whistle. This is called a pass back. The other team does a pass back to start the second half. Pass backs also occur at the center of the field after every goal.

The aim of field hockey is to score more goals than the other team. Players use their sticks to **dribble** or pass the ball up the field. While one team is moving the ball up the field toward the goal, the other team tries to take the ball away.

The team with the ball can try to score a goal when they are inside the other team's striking circle. The ball must pass over the goal line between the goal posts to count. Every goal is worth one point.

■ Field hockey players protect the ball from the other team by keeping their body between their opponents and the ball.

The player with the ball cannot shield the ball with their body or their stick. This is against the rules. It is called obstruction. A **foul** can also be called when a player lifts the curled edge of their stick above their shoulders. Players are also not allowed to hit the ball with their hands or use their body to stop the ball. **Stick interference** is also a foul. When a foul occurs within the striking circle, the umpire awards the opposite team a **penalty corner** or **penalty stroke**.

Each team has 10 players on the field and a goalie in outdoor field hockey. Games are divided into two periods of 30 minutes each for high school games. The two periods are 35 minutes each in college and international games.

Each team has five players on the field and a goalie in indoor field hockey. The game has two 30-minute periods.

Players are only allowed to hit the ball with the flat part of the stick. This side of the stick is also called the "face."

Offensive players dribble or pass the ball forward and try to score goals. Other players on the team defend their goal. They try to take the ball from the attackers on the other team.

Forwards play on the front line and attack the other team. Sometimes a coach puts five players on the forward line. Sometimes they will put three. A center forward plays in the middle. The two forwards on the outside are called wings. The two wings are the right wing and the left wing. Wings are also called outside-forwards. They help take the ball to the opposing side of the field and pass the ball to the center. When there are five players on the front line, the people in between the wings and center are called inners. The front line players all work together passing the ball back and forth. They also try to find ways to shoot and score on the opposing net.

Players must use their sticks to touch the ball. Goalies are the only players who are allowed to kick the ball.

Players called halfbacks, links, or midfielders play on the middle line. Players in this position have two key roles. They help their defense stop opponents. They also pass the ball to the forward line.

Defenders play on the back line. They are called fullbacks or backs. They help clear the ball from their goal area and attack the forwards on the opposite team. A defender who is chosen to always be the last person back is called a sweeper. The sweeper plays right in front of the goalie and helps defend the net. The sweeper helps block shots and **intercepts** the other team's plays.

■ Some defenders wear masks to protect their faces from hard shots from the other team's forwards.

Goalies block shots with their body, gloves, leg pads, and stick. They are not allowed to cover the ball. The goalie's jersey is a different color from the other players on the field.

■ Goalies wear padded equipment to protect the body when blocking shots.

I n North America, most field hockey players are female, but there are some men's teams. In some countries, such as India, Pakistan, the Netherlands, Germany, and Australia, field hockey is popular among males.

Field hockey is played by people of all ages. There are many youth leagues across the United States. Many high schools, colleges, and universities also have field hockey teams. They compete in **intercollegiate** tournaments and sometimes travel to other countries to compete. National teams play in tournaments around the world.

The Netherlands' women's field hockey team won the gold medal at the 2012 London Olympics. They defeated Argentina 2-0 in the final game.

The Olympic Games and the Federation of International Hockey (FIH) World Cup provide national teams with the chance to become world champions. Both competitions are held every four years. Twelve men's and women's field hockey teams compete in the Olympics. The top 12 men's and women's field hockey teams take part in the World Cup.

The United States has sent field hockey teams to the Pan American Games since the sport was first added to the men's program in 1967 and the women's program 20 years later. The Pan Am Games are always held during the summer before the Olympics.

The Champions Trophy Cup is a key annual field hockey tournament. The top eight teams in the world compete. The Commonwealth Games, the FIH Junior World Cup, and the U.S. National Hockey Festival are also key events. In the off-season, the National Indoor Tournament is the main event for U.S. field hockey players.

Australia won the gold medal at the FIH World Cup in 2010. They defeated Germany 2-1 in the gold medal game.

Field hockey attracts many types of athletes. Some prefer to play at the local club level, while others aim for international competition.

Beth Anders

BORN: November 13, 1951
REPRESENTED: United States
POSITION: Midfield

CAREER FACTS:

- Anders was on the national team from 1969 to 1980. She was the high scorer for the U.S. every year she was on the team.
- Her penalty corners were consistently recorded at speeds of 90 mph.
- She was the head coach at Old Dominion University for 30 seasons. She is the first Division I coach to reach 500 wins. Her team won the 2011 NCAA championship and have played in 29 NCAA tournaments.

Alyson Annan

BORN: June 21, 1973
REPRESENTED: Australia
POSITION: Forward

CAREER FACTS:

- Annan won the first FIH International Player of the Year award in 1998. She won the award again in 2000.
- She won Olympic gold medals with Australia in 1996 and 2000.
- Annan played in 228 games for Australia's national team. She scored 166 goals.

Teun de Nooijer

BORN: March 22, 1976
REPRESENTED: Netherlands
POSITION: Forward

CAREER FACTS:
- He was named FIH International Player of the Year in 2003, 2005, and 2006.
- De Nooijer won a gold medal in the 1996 and 2000 Olympic Games. He also won a silver medal at the 2004 and 2012 Olympic Games.
- De Nooijer has played more than 400 games with the Dutch national team. He has scored more than 200 goals.

Kate Barber

BORN: November 22, 1976
REPRESENTED: United States
EVENTS: Forward/Midfield

CAREER FACTS:
- She was named USA Field Hockey Female Athlete of the Year five times.
- She won three national championships when she played for the University of North Carolina.
- Barber's team won silver medals in both the 1999 Pan American Games and the 2001 Americas Cup. She was captain of the U.S. Olympic team in 2008.

Superstars of Field Hockey

Field hockey heroes of today inspire young athletes to try this exciting sport.

Luciana Aymar

BORN: August 10, 1977
REPRESENTS: Argentina
POSITION: Midfield

CAREER FACTS:

- Aymar was named the FIH International Player of the Year a record seven times: 2001, 2004, 2005, 2007, 2008, 2009, and 2010.
- She was named Player of the Tournament at the 2010 World Cup in her home country of Argentina.
- Her team has won two Olympic silver medals and two Olympic bronze medals. Her team has also won two World Cup trophies and a silver medal at the Pan American Games.

Jamie Dwyer

BORN: March 12, 1979
REPRESENTS: Australia
POSITION: Forward

CAREER FACTS:

- Dwyer was named the FIH International Player of the Year in 2004, 2007, 2009, 2010, and 2011.
- He won an Olympic gold medal in 2004. He also won a bronze medal in 2008 and 2012.
- Dwyer has played in more than 250 games for Australia. He is one of the team's captains and has scored more than 170 goals.

Tobias Hauke

BORN: September 11, 1987
REPRESENTS: Germany
POSITION: Defense

CAREER FACTS:
- Hauke was named the FIH Young International Player of the Year in 2010.
- He won a gold medal at the 2008 and 2012 Olympic Games.
- He made his debut for the German National Team in 2004.

Katie O'Donnell

BORN: December 6, 1988
REPRESENTS: United States
POSITION: Forward

CAREER FACTS:
- O'Donnell joined the U.S. National Team at 16. She was the youngest person ever to play for the team.
- O'Donnell was named the NCAA National Player of the Year in 2009 and 2010. She was named the USA National Team Athlete of the Year in 2010.
- She was named the Sportswoman of the Year in 2012 by the Women's Sports Foundation. Past winners of the award have included Mia Hamm and Venus Williams.

A Healthy Player

Field hockey is a fast-paced sport. Players need to be in top condition to perform well. Drinking plenty of water before, during, and after field hockey games is important. Players lose water from their bodies when they sweat during a game.

Eating healthy foods from all four food groups keeps field hockey players strong and full of energy. Grain products, fruits, and vegetables provide vitamins, minerals, and fiber for an athlete's body. Calcium in dairy products keeps bones strong. Meat, eggs, and other sources of protein build muscle.

■ When muscles work hard, they produce heat in the body. To keep cool, the body releases heat through sweat. Drinking water replaces the sweat.

■ It is important to eat 5 to 9 servings of vegetables a day.

Good field hockey players have speed, strength, and skill. **Conditioning** is an important part of training. It helps players breathe easier, avoid injuries, and run faster. Types of conditioning include stretching, weight training, **cardiovascular training**, and **agility training**.

Players should stretch before and after physical activity. This helps prepare them for running and helps reduce injuries. Many parts of the body should be stretched. This includes the legs, ankles, back, arms, shoulders, and neck.

Cardiovascular training, such as jogging and bicycling, help strengthen a player's heart and lungs. This is important because field hockey involves a lot running. Weight training builds strong muscles. Strong muscles help players hit the ball hard and run fast. Agility training improves a player's ball control, balance, and speed.

■ Field hockey players need to stretch both their upper body and their lower body before each game.

Field Hockey Brain Teasers

Test your field hockey knowledge by trying to answer these brain teasers!

1 How old is the game of field hockey?

2 Are field hockey players allowed to kick the ball?

3 Which player helps the goalie defend the goal cage?

4 Is field hockey only played outdoors?

5 What is it called when players try to shield the ball with their bodies?

6 What happens when a foul is called in the striking circle?

ANSWERS: 1. Field hockey dates back more than 4,000 years. 2. No, only goalies are allowed to kick the ball. 3. The sweeper helps the goalie. 4. In some countries, field hockey is also played indoors. 5. It is called obstruction. 6. The other team is awarded a penalty corner or penalty stroke.

Key Words

agility training: training that improves speed

cardiovascular training: training that improves breathing and heart rate

conditioning: exercising and eating well to make the body fit

dribble: control the ball with the stick while running down the field

foul: behavior that is against the rules

intercepts: stops a pass from the other team

intercollegiate: activities between two or more colleges

penalty corner: a free shot at the other team's goal taken from outside the striking circle. Several players on both teams are involved in the play

penalty stroke: a free shot at the other team's goal taken from at least 7 yards (6.4 m) out. Only the goalie and the shooter take part

stick interference: a foul called when a player brings his or her stick in contact with another player's stick

striking circles: semicircles on the field in front of the goal cages

umpire: a person who enforces the rules of the game

Index

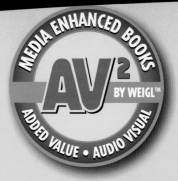

Log on to www.av2books.com

AV² by Weigl brings you media enhanced books that support active learning. Go to www.av2books.com, and enter the special code found on page 2 of this book. You will gain access to enriched and enhanced content that supplements and complements this book. Content includes video, audio, weblinks, quizzes, a slide show, and activities.

AV² Online Navigation

Audio
Listen to sect
the book rea

Book Pages
AV² pages directly correspond to pages in the book.

Video
Watch inform
video clips.

Embedded Web
Gain additional informa
for research.

Key Words
Study vocabulary, and complete a matching word activity.

Try This!
Complete activities and
hands-on experiments.

Quizzes
Test your knowledge.

Slide Show
View images and captions, and prepare a presentation.

AV² was built to bridge the gap between print and digital. We encourage you to tell us what you like and what you want to see in the future.

Sign up to be an AV² Ambassador at www.av2books.com/ambassador.

Due to the dynamic nature of the Internet, some of the URLs and activities provided as part of AV² by Weigl may have changed or ceased to exist. AV² by Weigl accepts no responsibility for any such changes. All media enhanced books are regularly monitored to update addresses and sites in a timely manner. Contact AV² by Weigl at 1-866-649-3445 or av2books@weigl.com with any questions, comments, or feedback.